NORTH

by the same author

poetry
DEATH OF A NATURALIST
DOOR INTO THE DARK
WINTERING OUT
FIELD WORK
SELECTED POEMS 1965–75
STATION ISLAND
SWEENEY ASTRAY
THE HAW LANTERN
THE RATTLE BAG
(*edited with Ted Hughes*)
NEW SELECTED POEMS 1966–1987
SEEING THINGS
SWEENEY'S FLIGHT
(*with Rachel Giese*)

prose
PREOCCUPATIONS:
Selected Prose 1968–78
THE GOVERNMENT OF THE TONGUE

plays
THE CURE AT TROY

SEAMUS HEANEY

North

faber and faber
LONDON · BOSTON

First published in Faber Paperbacks 1975
by Faber and Faber Limited
3 Queen Square London WCIN 3AU

Reprinted nine times
Reset 1992

Phototypeset by Wilmaset Ltd, Birkenhead, Wirral
Printed in England by Clays Ltd, St Ives plc
All rights reserved

A CIP record for this book is available
from the British Library

ISBN 0 571 10813 X

6 8 10 9 7 5

Contents

Acknowledgements, vii
Mossbawn:
Two Poems in Dedication for Mary Heaney, ix
   1 Sunlight, ix
   2 The Seed Cutters, xi

PART I

Antaeus, 3
Belderg, 4
Funeral Rites, 6
North, 10
Viking Dublin: Trial Pieces, 12
The Digging Skeleton, 17
Bone Dreams, 19
Come to the Bower, 24
Bog Queen, 25
The Grauballe Man, 28
Punishment, 30
Strange Fruit, 32
Kinship, 33
Ocean's Love to Ireland, 40
Aisling, 42
Act of Union, 43
The Betrothal of Cavehill, 45
Hercules and Antaeus, 46

PART II

The Unacknowledged Legislator's Dream, 50
Whatever You Say Say Nothing, 51
Freedman, 55
Singing School, 56
   1 The Ministry of Fear, 57
   2 A Constable Calls, 60
   3 Orange Drums, Tyrone, 1966, 62
   4 Summer 1969, 63
   5 Fosterage, 65
   6 Exposure, 66

Acknowledgements

The author gratefully acknowledges the assistance of the American Irish Foundation during 1973/4 when he was recipient of their annual Literary Award.

Acknowledgements are due to the editors of the following where some of these poems appeared for the first time: *Antaeus, The Arts in Ireland, Causeway* (BBC Radio 3), *Encounter, Exile, Hibernia, The Irish Press, The Irish Times, Irish University Review, James Joyce Quarterly, The Listener, The New Review, Phoenix, The Times Literary Supplement*; and to the editors of the following anthologies: *The Faber Book of Irish Verse, New Poems 1972–1973* and *New Poems 1973–1974* (Hutchinson), and *Soundings '72* (Blackstaff, Belfast).

Eight of the poems appeared in a limited edition entitled *Bog Poems* (Rainbow Press).

Mossbawn: Two Poems
in Dedication

for Mary Heaney

I. SUNLIGHT

There was a sunlit absence.
The helmeted pump in the yard
heated its iron,
water honeyed

in the slung bucket
and the sun stood
like a griddle cooling
against the wall

of each long afternoon.
So, her hands scuffled
over the bakeboard,
the reddening stove

sent its plaque of heat
against her where she stood
in a floury apron
by the window.

Now she dusts the board
with a goose's wing,
now sits, broad-lapped,
with whitened nails

and measling shins:
here is a space
again, the scone rising
to the tick of two clocks.

And here is love
like a tinsmith's scoop
sunk past its gleam
in the meal-bin.

2. THE SEED CUTTERS

They seem hundreds of years away. Breughel,
You'll know them if I can get them true.
They kneel under the hedge in a half-circle
Behind a windbreak wind is breaking through.
They are the seed cutters. The tuck and frill
Of leaf-sprout is on the seed potatoes
Buried under that straw. With time to kill
They are taking their time. Each sharp knife goes
Lazily halving each root that falls apart
In the palm of the hand: a milky gleam,
And, at the centre, a dark watermark.
O calendar customs! Under the broom
Yellowing over them, compose the frieze
With all of us there, our anonymities.

PART I

Antaeus

When I lie on the ground
I rise flushed as a rose in the morning.
In fights I arrange a fall on the ring
  To rub myself with sand

That is operative
As an elixir. I cannot be weaned
Off the earth's long contour, her river-veins.
  Down here in my cave,

Girded with root and rock,
I am cradled in the dark that wombed me
And nurtured in every artery
  Like a small hillock.

Let each new hero come
Seeking the golden apples and Atlas.
He must wrestle with me before he pass
  Into that realm of fame

Among sky-born and royal:
He may well throw me and renew my birth
But let him not plan, lifting me off the earth,
  My elevation, my fall.

1966

[3]

Belderg

'They just kept turning up
And were thought of as foreign' –
One-eyed and benign
They lie about his house,
Quernstones out of a bog.

To lift the lid of the peat
And find this pupil dreaming
Of neolithic wheat!
When he stripped off blanket bog
The soft-piled centuries

Fell open like a glib:
There were the first plough-marks,
The stone-age fields, the tomb
Corbelled, turfed and chambered,
Floored with dry turf-coomb.

A landscape fossilized,
Its stone-wall patternings
Repeated before our eyes
In the stone walls of Mayo.
Before I turned to go

He talked about persistence,
A congruence of lives,
How, stubbed and cleared of stones,
His home accrued growth rings
Of iron, flint and bronze.

So I talked of Mossbawn,
A bogland name. 'But *moss*?'
He crossed my old home's music
With older strains of Norse.
I'd told how its foundation

Was mutable as sound
And how I could derive
A forked root from that ground
And make *bawn* an English fort,
A planter's walled-in mound,

Or else find sanctuary
And think of it as Irish,
Persistent if outworn.
'But the Norse ring on your tree?'
I passed through the eye of the quern,

Grist to an ancient mill,
And in my mind's eye saw
A world-tree of balanced stones,
Querns piled like vertebrae,
The marrow crushed to grounds.

Funeral Rites

I

I shouldered a kind of manhood,
stepping in to lift the coffins
of dead relations.
They had been laid out

in tainted rooms,
their eyelids glistening,
their dough-white hands
shackled in rosary beads.

Their puffed knuckles
had unwrinkled, the nails
were darkened, the wrists
obediently sloped.

The dulse-brown shroud,
the quilted satin cribs:
I knelt courteously,
admiring it all,

as wax melted down
and veined the candles,
the flames hovering
to the women hovering

behind me.
And always, in a corner,
the coffin lid,
its nail-heads dressed

with little gleaming crosses.
Dear soapstone masks,
kissing their igloo brows
had to suffice

before the nails were sunk
and the black glacier
of each funeral
pushed away.

II

Now as news comes in
of each neighbourly murder
we pine for ceremony,
customary rhythms:

the temperate footsteps
of a cortège, winding past
each blinded home.
I would restore

the great chambers of Boyne,
prepare a sepulchre
under the cupmarked stones.
Out of side-streets and bye-roads

purring family cars
nose into line,
the whole country tunes
to the muffled drumming

of ten thousand engines.
Somnambulant women,
left behind, move
through emptied kitchens

imagining our slow triumph
towards the mounds.
Quiet as a serpent
in its grassy boulevard,

the procession drags its tail
out of the Gap of the North
as its head already enters
the megalithic doorway.

III

When they have put the stone
back in its mouth
we will drive north again
past Strang and Carling fjords,

the cud of memory
allayed for once, arbitration
of the feud placated,
imagining those under the hill

[8]

disposed like Gunnar
who lay beautiful
inside his burial mound,
though dead by violence

and unavenged.
Men said that he was chanting
verses about honour
and that four lights burned

in corners of the chamber:
which opened then, as he turned
with a joyful face
to look at the moon.

North

I returned to a long strand,
the hammered shod of a bay,
and found only the secular
powers of the Atlantic thundering.

I faced the unmagical
invitations of Iceland,
the pathetic colonies
of Greenland, and suddenly

those fabulous raiders,
those lying in Orkney and Dublin
measured against
their long swords rusting,

those in the solid
belly of stone ships,
those hacked and glinting
in the gravel of thawed streams

were ocean-deafened voices
warning me, lifted again
in violence and epiphany.
The longship's swimming tongue

was buoyant with hindsight —
it said Thor's hammer swung
to geography and trade,
thick-witted couplings and revenges,

the hatreds and behindbacks
of the althing, lies and women,
exhaustions nominated peace,
memory incubating the spilled blood.

It said, 'Lie down
in the word-hoard, burrow
the coil and gleam
of your furrowed brain.

Compose in darkness.
Expect aurora borealis
in the long foray
but no cascade of light.

Keep your eye clear
as the bleb of the icicle,
trust the feel of what nubbed treasure
your hands have known.'

Viking Dublin: Trial Pieces

I

It could be a jaw-bone
or a rib or a portion cut
from something sturdier:
anyhow, a small outline

was incised, a cage
or trellis to conjure in.
Like a child's tongue
following the toils

of his calligraphy,
like an eel swallowed
in a basket of eels,
the line amazes itself,

eluding the hand
that fed it,
a bill in flight,
a swimming nostril.

II

These are trial pieces,
the craft's mystery
improvised on bone:
foliage, bestiaries,

interlacings elaborate
as the netted routes
of ancestry and trade.
That have to be

magnified on display
so that the nostril
is a migrant prow
sniffing the Liffey,

swanning it up to the ford,
dissembling itself
in antler combs, bone pins,
coins, weights, scale-pans.

III

Like a long sword
sheathed in its moisting
burial clays,
the keel stuck fast

in the slip of the bank,
its clinker-built hull
spined and plosive
as *Dublin*.

And now we reach in
for shards of the vertebrae,
the ribs of hurdle,
the mother-wet caches —

and for this trial piece
incised by a child,
a longship, a buoyant
migrant line.

IV

That enters my longhand,
turns cursive, unscarfing
a zoomorphic wake,
a worm of thought

I follow into the mud.
I am Hamlet the Dane,
skull-handler, parablist,
smeller of rot

in the state, infused
with its poisons,
pinioned by ghosts
and affections,

murders and pieties,
coming to consciousness
by jumping in graves,
dithering, blathering.

V

Come fly with me,
come sniff the wind
with the expertise
of the Vikings –

neighbourly, scoretaking
killers, haggers
and hagglers, gombeen-men,
hoarders of grudges and gain.

With a butcher's aplomb
they spread out your lungs
and made you warm wings
for your shoulders.

Old fathers, be with us.
Old cunning assessors
of feuds and of sites
for ambush or town.

VI

'Did you ever hear tell,'
said Jimmy Farrell,
'of the skulls they have
in the city of Dublin?

White skulls and black skulls
and yellow skulls, and some
with full teeth, and some
haven't only but one,'

and compounded history
in the pan of 'an old Dane,
maybe, was drowned
in the Flood.'

My words lick around
cobbled quays, go hunting
lightly as pampooties
over the skull-capped ground.

The Digging Skeleton

After Baudelaire

I

You find anatomical plates
Buried along these dusty quays
Among books yellowed like mummies
Slumbering in forgotten crates,

Drawings touched with an odd beauty
As if the illustrator had
Responded gravely to the sad
Mementoes of anatomy –

Mysterious candid studies
Of red slobland around the bones.
Like this one: flayed men and skeletons
Digging the earth like navvies.

II

Sad gang of apparitions,
Your skinned muscles like plaited sedge
And your spines hooped towards the sunk edge
Of the spade, my patient ones,

Tell me, as you labour hard
To break this unrelenting soil,
What barns are there for you to fill?
What farmer dragged you from the boneyard?

Or are you emblems of the truth,
Death's lifers, hauled from the narrow cell
And stripped of night-shirt shrouds, to tell:
'This is the reward of faith

In rest eternal. Even death
Lies. The void deceives.
We do not fall like autumn leaves
To sleep in peace. Some traitor breath

Revives our clay, sends us abroad
And by the sweat of our stripped brows
We earn our deaths; our one repose
When the bleeding instep finds its spade.'

Bone Dreams

I

White bone found
on the grazing:
the rough, porous
language of touch

and its yellowing, ribbed
impression in the grass —
a small ship-burial.
As dead as stone,

flint-find, nugget
of chalk,
I touch it again,
I wind it in

the sling of mind
to pitch it at England
and follow its drop
to strange fields.

II

Bone-house:
a skeleton
in the tongue's
old dungeons.

I push back
through dictions,
Elizabethan canopies.
Norman devices,

the erotic mayflowers
of Provence
and the ivied latins
of churchmen

to the scop's
twang, the iron
flash of consonants
cleaving the line.

III

In the coffered
riches of grammar
and declensions
I found *ban-bus*,

its fire, benches,
wattle and rafters,
where the soul
fluttered a while

in the roofspace.
There was a small crock
for the brain,
and a cauldron

of generation
swung at the centre:
love-den, blood-holt,
dream-bower.

IV

Come back past
philology and kennings,
re-enter memory
where the bone's lair

is a love-nest
in the grass.
I hold my lady's head
like a crystal

and ossify myself
by gazing: I am screes
on her escarpments,
a chalk giant

carved upon her downs.
Soon my hands, on the sunken
fosse of her spine
move towards the passes.

V

And we end up
cradling each other
between the lips
of an earthwork.

As I estimate
for pleasure
her knuckles' paving,
the turning stiles

of the elbows,
the vallum of her brow
and the long wicket
of collar-bone,

I have begun to pace
the Hadrian's Wall
of her shoulder, dreaming
of Maiden Castle.

VI

One morning in Devon
I found a dead mole
with the dew still beading it.
I had thought the mole

a big-boned coulter
but there it was
small and cold
as the thick of a chisel.

I was told 'Blow,
blow back the fur on his head.
Those little points
were the eyes.

And feel the shoulders.'
I touched small distant Pennines,
a pelt of grass and grain
running south.

Come to the Bower

My hands come, touched
By sweetbriar and tangled vetch,
Foraging past the burst gizzards
Of coin-hoards

To where the dark-bowered queen,
Whom I unpin,
Is waiting. Out of the black maw
Of the peat, sharpened willow

Withdraws gently.
I unwrap skins and see
The pot of the skull,
The damp tuck of each curl

Reddish as a fox's brush,
A mark of a gorget in the flesh
Of her throat. And spring water
Starts to rise around her.

I reach past
The riverbed's washed
Dream of gold to the bullion
Of her Venus bone.

Bog Queen

I lay waiting
between turf-face and demesne wall,
between heathery levels
and glass-toothed stone.

My body was braille
for the creeping influences:
dawn suns groped over my head
and cooled at my feet,

through my fabrics and skins
the seeps of winter
digested me,
the illiterate roots

pondered and died
in the cavings
of stomach and socket.
I lay waiting

on the gravel bottom,
my brain darkening,
a jar of spawn
fermenting underground

dreams of Baltic amber.
Bruised berries under my nails,
the vital hoard reducing
in the crock of the pelvis.

My diadem grew carious,
gemstones dropped
in the peat floe
like the bearings of history.

My sash was a black glacier
wrinkling, dyed weaves
and phoenician stitchwork
retted on my breasts'

soft moraines.
I knew winter cold
like the nuzzle of fjords
at my thighs –

the soaked fledge, the heavy
swaddle of hides.
My skull hibernated
in the wet nest of my hair.

Which they robbed.
I was barbered
and stripped
by a turfcutter's spade

who veiled me again
and packed coomb softly
between the stone jambs
at my head and my feet.

Till a peer's wife bribed him.
The plait of my hair,
a slimy birth-cord
of bog, had been cut

and I rose from the dark,
hacked bone, skull-ware,
frayed stitches, tufts,
small gleams on the bank.

The Grauballe Man

As if he had been poured
in tar, he lies
on a pillow of turf
and seems to weep

the black river of himself.
The grain of his wrists
is like bog oak,
the ball of his heel

like a basalt egg.
His instep has shrunk
cold as a swan's foot
or a wet swamp root.

His hips are the ridge
and purse of a mussel,
his spine an eel arrested
under a glisten of mud.

The head lifts,
the chin is a visor
raised above the vent
of his slashed throat

that has tanned and toughened.
The cured wound
opens inwards to a dark
elderberry place.

Who will say 'corpse'
to his vivid cast?
Who will say 'body'
to his opaque repose?

And his rusted hair,
a mat unlikely
as a foetus's.
I first saw his twisted face

in a photograph,
a head and shoulder
out of the peat,
bruised like a forceps baby,

but now he lies
perfected in my memory,
down to the red horn
of his nails,

hung in the scales
with beauty and atrocity:
with the Dying Gaul
too strictly compassed

on his shield,
with the actual weight
of each hooded victim,
slashed and dumped.

Punishment

I can feel the tug
of the halter at the nape
of her neck, the wind
on her naked front.

It blows her nipples
to amber beads,
it shakes the frail rigging
of her ribs.

I can see her drowned
body in the bog,
the weighing stone,
the floating rods and boughs.

Under which at first
she was a barked sapling
that is dug up
oak-bone, brain-firkin:

her shaved head
like a stubble of black corn,
her blindfold a soiled bandage,
her noose a ring

to store
the memories of love.
Little adulteress,
before they punished you

you were flaxen-haired,
undernourished, and your
tar-black face was beautiful.
My poor scapegoat,

I almost love you
but would have cast, I know,
the stones of silence.
I am the artful voyeur

of your brain's exposed
and darkened combs,
your muscles' webbing
and all your numbered bones:

I who have stood dumb
when your betraying sisters,
cauled in tar,
wept by the railings,

who would connive
in civilized outrage
yet understand the exact
and tribal, intimate revenge.

Strange Fruit

Here is the girl's head like an exhumed gourd.
Oval-faced, prune-skinned, prune-stones for teeth.
They unswaddled the wet fern of her hair
And made an exhibition of its coil,
Let the air at her leathery beauty.
Pash of tallow, perishable treasure:
Her broken nose is dark as a turf clod,
Her eyeholes blank as pools in the old workings.
Diodorus Siculus confessed
His gradual ease among the likes of this:
Murdered, forgotten, nameless, terrible
Beheaded girl, outstaring axe
And beatification, outstaring
What had begun to feel like reverence.

Kinship

I

Kinned by hieroglyphic
peat on a spreadfield
to the strangled victim,
the love-nest in the bracken,

I step through origins
like a dog turning
its memories of wilderness
on the kitchen mat:

the bog floor shakes,
water cheeps and lisps
as I walk down
rushes and heather.

I love this turf-face,
its black incisions,
the cooped secrets
of process and ritual;

I love the spring
off the ground,
each bank a gallows drop,
each open pool

the unstopped mouth
of an urn, a moon-drinker,
not to be sounded
by the naked eye.

II

Quagmire, swampland, morass:
the slime kingdoms,
domains of the cold-blooded,
of mud pads and dirtied eggs.

But *bog*
meaning soft,
the fall of windless rain,
pupil of amber.

Ruminant ground,
digestion of mollusc
and seed-pod,
deep pollen-bin.

Earth-pantry, bone vault,
sun-bank, embalmer
of votive goods
and sabred fugitives.

Insatiable bride.
Sword-swallower,
casket, midden,
floe of history.

Ground that will strip
its dark side,
nesting ground,
outback of my mind.

III

I found a turf-spade
hidden under bracken,
laid flat, and overgrown
with a green fog.

As I raised it
the soft lips of the growth
muttered and split,
a tawny rut

opening at my feet
like a shed skin,
the shaft wettish
as I sank it upright

and beginning to
steam in the sun.
And now they have twinned
that obelisk:

among the stones,
under a bearded cairn
a love-nest is disturbed,
catkin and bog-cotton tremble

as they raise up
the cloven oak-limb.
I stand at the edge of centuries
facing a goddess.

IV

This centre holds
and spreads,
sump and seedbed,
a bag of waters

and a melting grave.
The mothers of autumn
sour and sink,
ferments of husk and leaf

deepen their ochres.
Mosses come to a head,
heather unseeds,
brackens deposit

their bronze.
This is the vowel of earth
dreaming its root
in flowers and snow,

mutation of weathers
and seasons,
a windfall composing
the floor it rots into.

I grew out of all this
like a weeping willow
inclined to
the appetites of gravity.

v

The hand-carved felloes
of the turf-cart wheels
buried in a litter
of turf mould,

the cupid's bow
of the tail-board,
the socketed lips
of the cribs:

I deified the man
who rode there,
god of the waggon,
the hearth-feeder.

I was his privileged
attendant, a bearer
of bread and drink,
the squire of his circuits.

When summer died
and wives forsook the fields
we were abroad,
saluted, given right-of-way.

Watch our progress
down the haw-lit hedges,
my manly pride
when he speaks to me.

VI

And you, Tacitus,
observe how I make my grove
on an old crannog
piled by the fearful dead:

a desolate peace.
Our mother ground
is sour with the blood
of her faithful,

they lie gargling
in her sacred heart
as the legions stare
from the ramparts.

Come back to this
'island of the ocean'
where nothing will suffice.
Read the inhumed faces

of casualty and victim;
report us fairly,
how we slaughter
for the common good

and shave the heads
of the notorious,
how the goddess swallows
our love and terror.

Ocean's Love to Ireland

Speaking broad Devonshire,
Ralegh has backed the maid to a tree
As Ireland is backed to England

And drives inland
Till all her strands are breathless:
'Sweesir, Swatter! Sweesir, Swatter!'

He is water, he is ocean, lifting
Her farthingale like a scarf of weed lifting
In the front of a wave.

II

Yet his superb crest inclines to Cynthia
Even while it runs its bent
In the rivers of Lee and Blackwater.

Those are the plashy spots where he would lay
His cape before her. In London, his name
Will rise on water, and on these dark seepings:

Smerwick sowed with the mouthing corpses
Of six hundred papists, 'as gallant and good
Personages as ever were beheld.'

The ruined maid complains in Irish,
Ocean has scattered her dreams of fleets,
The Spanish prince has spilled his gold

And failed her. Iambic drums
Of English beat the woods where her poets
Sink like Onan. Rush-light, mushroom-flesh,

She fades from their somnolent clasp
Into ringlet-breath and dew,
The ground possessed and repossessed.

Aisling

He courted her
With a decadent sweet art
Like the wind's vowel
Blowing through the hazels:

'Are you Diana . . . ?'
And was he Actaeon,
His high lament
The stag's exhausted belling?

Act of Union

I

To-night, a first movement, a pulse,
As if the rain in bogland gathered head
To slip and flood: a bog-burst,
A gash breaking open the ferny bed.
Your back is a firm line of eastern coast
And arms and legs are thrown
Beyond your gradual hills. I caress
The heaving province where our past has grown.
I am the tall kingdom over your shoulder
That you would neither cajole nor ignore.
Conquest is a lie. I grow older
Conceding your half-independent shore
Within whose borders now my legacy
Culminates inexorably.

II

And I am still imperially
Male, leaving you with the pain,
The rending process in the colony,
The battering ram, the boom burst from within.
The act sprouted an obstinate fifth column
Whose stance is growing unilateral.
His heart beneath your heart is a wardrum
Mustering force. His parasitical
And ignorant little fists already
Beat at your borders and I know they're cocked
At me across the water. No treaty

I foresee will salve completely your tracked
And stretchmarked body, the big pain
That leaves you raw, like opened ground, again.

The Betrothal of Cavehill

Gunfire barks its questions off Cavehill
And the profiled basalt maintains its stare
South: proud, protestant and northern, and male.
Adam untouched, before the shock of gender.

They still shoot here for luck over a bridegroom.
The morning I drove out to bed me down
Among my love's hideouts, her pods and broom,
They fired above my car the ritual gun.

Hercules and Antaeus

Sky-born and royal,
snake-choker, dung-heaver,
his mind big with golden apples,
his future hung with trophies,

Hercules has the measure
of resistance and black powers
feeding off the territory.
Antaeus, the mould-hugger,

is weaned at last:
a fall was a renewal
but now he is raised up –
the challenger's intelligence

is a spur of light,
a blue prong graiping him
out of his element
into a dream of loss

and origins – the cradling dark,
the river-veins, the secret gullies
of his strength,
the hatching grounds

of cave and souterrain,
he has bequeathed it all
to elegists. Balor will die
and Byrthnoth and Sitting Bull.

Hercules lifts his arms
in a remorseless V,
his triumph unassailed
by the powers he has shaken,

and lifts and banks Antaeus
high as a profiled ridge,
a sleeping giant,
pap for the dispossessed.

PART II

The Unacknowledged
Legislator's Dream

Archimedes thought he could move the world if he could find the right place to position his lever. Billy Hunter said Tarzan shook the world when he jumped down out of a tree.

I sink my crowbar in a chink I know under the masonry of state and statute, I swing on a creeper of secrets into the Bastille. My wronged people cheer from their cages. The guard-dogs are unmuzzled, a soldier pivots a muzzle at the butt of my ear, I am stood blindfolded with my hands above my head until I seem to be swinging from a strappado.

The commandant motions me to be seated. 'I am honoured to add a poet to our list.' He is amused and genuine. 'You'll be safer here, anyhow.'

In the cell, I wedge myself with outstretched arms in the corner and heave, I jump on the concrete flags to test them. Were those your eyes just now at the hatch?

Whatever You Say
Say Nothing

I

I'm writing just after an encounter
With an English journalist in search of 'views
On the Irish thing'. I'm back in winter
Quarters where bad news is no longer news,

Where media-men and stringers sniff and point,
Where zoom lenses, recorders and coiled leads
Litter the hotels. The times are out of joint
But I incline as much to rosary beads

As to the jottings and analyses
Of politicians and newspapermen
Who've scribbled down the long campaign from gas
And protest to gelignite and sten,

Who proved upon their pulses 'escalate',
'Backlash' and 'crack down', 'the provisional wing',
'Polarization' and 'long-standing hate'.
Yet I live here, I live here too, I sing,

Expertly civil-tongued with civil neighbours
On the high wires of first wireless reports,
Sucking the fake taste, the stony flavours
Of those sanctioned, old, elaborate retorts:

'Oh, it's disgraceful, surely, I agree,'
'Where's it going to end?' 'It's getting worse.'
'They're murderers,' 'Internment, understandably . . .'
The 'voice of sanity' is getting hoarse.

II

Men die at hand. In blasted street and home
The gelignite's a common sound effect:
As the man said when Celtic won, 'The Pope of Rome
's a happy man this night.' His flock suspect

In their deepest heart of hearts the heretic
Has come at last to heel and to the stake.
We tremble near the flames but want no truck
With the actual firing. We're on the make

As ever. Long sucking the hind tit
Cold as a witch's and as hard to swallow
Still leaves us fork-tongued on the border bit:
The liberal papist note sounds hollow

When amplified and mixed in with the bangs
That shake all hearts and windows day and night.
(It's tempting here to rhyme on 'labour pangs'
And diagnose a rebirth in our plight

But that would be to ignore other symptoms.
Last night you didn't need a stethoscope
To hear the eructation of Orange drums
Allergic equally to Pearse and Pope.)

On all sides 'little platoons' are mustering –
The phrase is Cruise O'Brien's via that great
Backlash, Burke – while I sit here with a pestering
Drouth for words at once both gaff and bait

To lure the tribal shoals to epigram
And order. I believe any of us
Could draw the line through bigotry and sham,
Given the right line, *aere perennius*.

III

'Religion's never mentioned here,' of course.
'You know them by their eyes,' and hold your tongue.
'One side's as bad as the other,' never worse.
Christ, it's near time that some small leak was sprung

In the great dykes the Dutchman made
To dam the dangerous tide that followed Seamus.
Yet for all this art and sedentary trade
I am incapable. The famous

Northern reticence, the tight gag of place
And times: yes, yes. Of the 'wee six' I sing
Where to be saved you only must save face
And whatever you say, you say nothing.

Smoke-signals are loud-mouthed compared with us:
Manoeuvrings to find out name and school,
Subtle discrimination by addresses
With hardly an exception to the rule

That Norman, Ken and Sidney signalled Prod,
And Seamus (call me Sean) was sure-fire Pape.
O land of password, handgrip, wink and nod,
Of open minds as open as a trap,

Where tongues lie coiled, as under flames lie wicks,
Where half of us, as in a wooden horse
Were cabin'd and confined like wily Greeks,
Besieged within the siege, whispering morse.

IV

This morning from a dewy motorway
I saw the new camp for the internees:
A bomb had left a crater of fresh clay
In the roadside, and over in the trees

Machine-gun posts defined a real stockade.
There was that white mist you get on a low ground
And it was déjà-vu, some film made
Of Stalag 17, a bad dream with no sound.

Is there a life before death? That's chalked up
In Ballymurphy. Competence with pain,
Coherent miseries, a bite and sup,
We hug our little destiny again.

Freedman

Indeed, slavery comes nearest to its justification in the early Roman Empire: for a man from a 'backward' race might be brought within the pale of civilization, educated and trained in a craft or a profession, and turned into a useful member of society.

R. H. BARROW: THE ROMANS

Subjugated yearly under arches,
Manumitted by parchments and degrees,
My murex was the purple dye of lents
On calendars all fast and abstinence.

'*Memento homo quia pulvis es.*'
I would kneel to be impressed by ashes,
A silk friction, a light stipple of dust –
I was under the thumb too like all my caste.

One of the earth-starred denizens, indelibly,
I sought the mark in vain on the groomed optimi:
Their estimating, census-taking eyes
Fastened on my mouldy brow like lampreys.

Then poetry arrived in that city –
I would abjure all cant and self-pity –
And poetry wiped my brow and sped me.
Now they will say I bite the hand that fed me.

Singing School

Fair seedtime had my soul, and I grew up
Fostered alike by beauty and by fear;
Much favoured in my birthplace, and no less
In that beloved Vale to which, erelong,
I was transplanted . . .
  WILLIAM WORDSWORTH: THE PRELUDE

He [the stable-boy] had a book of Orange rhymes, and
the days when we read them together in the hay-loft
gave me the pleasure of rhyme for the first time. Later
on I can remember being told, when there was a
rumour of a Fenian rising, that rifles were being
handed out to the Orangemen; and presently, when I
began to dream of my future life, I thought I would
like to die fighting the Fenians.
  W. B. YEATS: AUTOBIOGRAPHIES

I. THE MINISTRY OF FEAR

For Seamus Deane

Well, as Kavanagh said, we have lived
In important places. The lonely scarp
Of St Columb's College, where I billeted
For six years, overlooked your Bogside.
I gazed into new worlds: the inflamed throat
Of Brandywell, its floodlit dogtrack,
The throttle of the hare. In the first week
I was so homesick I couldn't even eat
The biscuits left to sweeten my exile.
I threw them over the fence one night
In September 1951
When the lights of houses in the Lecky Road
Were amber in the fog. It was an act
Of stealth.
            Then Belfast, and then Berkeley.
Here's two on's are sophisticated,
Dabbling in verses till they have become
A life: from bulky envelopes arriving
In vacation time to slim volumes
Despatched 'with the author's compliments'.
Those poems in longhand, ripped from the wire spine
Of your exercise-book, bewildered me —
Vowels and ideas bandied free
As the seed-pots blowing off our sycamores.
I tried to write about the sycamores
And innovated a South Derry rhyme
With *hushed* and *lulled* full chimes for *pushed* and *pulled*.
Those hobnailed boots from beyond the mountain

Were walking, by God, all over the fine
Lawns of elocution.

              Have our accents
Changed? 'Catholics, in general, don't speak
As well as students from the Protestant schools.'
Remember that stuff? Inferiority
Complexes, stuff that dreams were made on.
'What's your name, Heaney?'

                           'Heaney, Father.'

                                 'Fair
Enough.'

        On my first day, the leather strap
Went epileptic in the Big Study,
Its echoes plashing over our bowed heads,
But I still wrote home that a boarder's life
Was not so bad, shying as usual.

On long vacations, then, I came to life
In the kissing seat of an Austin Sixteen
Parked at a gable, the engine running,
My fingers tight as ivy on her shoulders,
A light left burning for her in the kitchen.
And heading back for home, the summer's
Freedom dwindling night by night, the air
All moonlight and a scent of hay, policemen
Swung their crimson flashlamps, crowding round
The car like black cattle, snuffing and pointing
The muzzle of a sten-gun in my eye:
'What's your name, driver?'

                        'Seamus . . .'

                            Seamus?

They once read my letters at a roadblock
And shone their torches on your hieroglyphics,
'Svelte dictions' in a very florid hand.

Ulster was British, but with no rights on
The English lyric: all around us, though
We hadn't named it, the ministry of fear.

2. A CONSTABLE CALLS

His bicycle stood at the window-sill,
The rubber cowl of a mud-splasher
Skirting the front mudguard,
Its fat black handlegrips

Heating in sunlight, the 'spud'
Of the dynamo gleaming and cocked back,
The pedal treads hanging relieved
Of the boot of the law.

His cap was upside down
On the floor, next his chair.
The line of its pressure ran like a bevel
In his slightly sweating hair.

He had unstrapped
The heavy ledger, and my father
Was making tillage returns
In acres, roods, and perches.

Arithmetic and fear.
I sat staring at the polished holster
With its buttoned flap, the braid cord
Looped into the revolver butt.

'Any other root crops?
Mangolds? Marrowstems? Anything like that?'
'No.' But was there not a line
Of turnips where the seed ran out

In the potato field? I assumed
Small guilts and sat
Imagining the black hole in the barracks.
He stood up, shifted the baton-case

Further round on his belt,
Closed the domesday book,
Fitted his cap back with two hands,
And looked at me as he said goodbye.

A shadow bobbed in the window.
He was snapping the carrier spring
Over the ledger. His boot pushed off
And the bicycle ticked, ticked, ticked.

3. ORANGE DRUMS, TYRONE, 1966

The lambeg balloons at his belly, weighs
Him back on his haunches, lodging thunder
Grossly there between his chin and his knees.
He is raised up by what he buckles under.

Each arm extended by a seasoned rod,
He parades behind it. And though the drummers
Are granted passage through the nodding crowd,
It is the drums preside, like giant tumours.

To every cocked ear, expert in its greed,
His battered signature subscribes 'No Pope'.
The goatskin's sometimes plastered with his blood.
The air is pounding like a stethoscope.

4. SUMMER 1969

While the Constabulary covered the mob
Firing into the Falls, I was suffering
Only the bullying sun of Madrid.
Each afternoon, in the casserole heat
Of the flat, as I sweated my way through
The life of Joyce, stinks from the fishmarket
Rose like the reek off a flax-dam.
At night on the balcony, gules of wine,
A sense of children in their dark corners,
Old women in black shawls near open windows,
The air a canyon rivering in Spanish.
We talked our way home over starlit plains
Where patent leather of the Guardia-Civil
Gleamed like fish-bellies in flax-poisoned waters.

'Go back,' one said, 'try to touch the people.'
Another conjured Lorca from his hill.
We sat through death-counts and bullfight reports
On the television, celebrities
Arrived from where the real thing still happened.

I retreated to the cool of the Prado.
Goya's 'Shootings of the Third of May'
Covered a wall – the thrown-up arms
And spasm of the rebel, the helmeted
And knapsacked military, the efficient
Rake of the fusillade. In the next room,
His nightmares, grafted to the palace wall –
Dark cyclones, hosting, breaking; Saturn

Jewelled in the blood of his own children;
Gigantic Chaos turning his brute hips
Over the world. Also, that holmgang
Where two berserks club each other to death
For honour's sake, greaved in a bog, and sinking.

He painted with his fists and elbows, flourished
The stained cape of his heart as history charged.

5. FOSTERAGE

For Michael McLaverty

'Description is revelation!' Royal
Avenue, Belfast, 1962,
A Saturday afternoon, glad to meet
Me, newly cubbed in language, he gripped
My elbow. 'Listen. Go your own way.
Do your own work. Remember
Katherine Mansfield – *I will tell*
How the laundry basket squeaked . . . that note of
   exile.'
But to hell with overstating it:
'Don't have the veins bulging in your biro.'
And then, 'Poor Hopkins!' I have the *Journals*
He gave me, underlined, his buckled self
Obeisant to their pain. He discerned
The lineaments of patience everywhere
And fostered me and sent me out, with words
Imposing on my tongue like obols.

6. EXPOSURE

It is December in Wicklow:
Alders dripping, birches
Inheriting the last light,
The ash tree cold to look at.

A comet that was lost
Should be visible at sunset,
Those million tons of light
Like a glimmer of haws and rose-hips,

And I sometimes see a falling star.
If I could come on meteorite!
Instead I walk through damp leaves,
Husks, the spent flukes of autumn,

Imagining a hero
On some muddy compound,
His gift like a slingstone
Whirled for the desperate.

How did I end up like this?
I often think of my friends'
Beautiful prismatic counselling
And the anvil brains of some who hate me

As I sit weighing and weighing
My responsible *tristia*.
For what? For the ear? For the people?
For what is said behind-backs?

Rain comes down through the alders,
Its low conducive voices
Mutter about let-downs and erosions
And yet each drop recalls

The diamond absolutes.
I am neither internee nor informer;
An inner émigré, grown long-haired
And thoughtful; a wood-kerne

Escaped from the massacre,
Taking protective colouring
From bole and bark, feeling
Every wind that blows;

Who, blowing up these sparks
For their meagre heat, have missed
The once-in-a-lifetime portent,
The comet's pulsing rose.